Wind In the Aspens

Gina Browning

Plain View Press
P.O. 42255
Austin, TX 78704

plainviewpress.net
pk@plainviewpress.net
512-441-2452

Copyright © 2011 Gina Browning. All rights reserved under International and Pan-American Copyright Conventions. No part of this book may be reproduced or distributed in any form or by any means, or stored in a data base or retrieval system, without written permission from the author. All rights, including electronic, are reserved by the author and publisher.

ISBN: 978-1-935514-60-2
Library of Congress Number: 2010936485

Edited by Ellen Kleiner
Design concept by Janice St. Marie
Cover photo by Brad Wilson

*To my parents, Jinny and Larry,
whose front door was always open during my childhood,
allowing friends, ideas, and love to enter.
Through their love and support, I learned to fearlessly trust this life
and to approach each moment with fullness.
Their wisdom, humanity, and generosity of spirit
continue to inspire me.*

*To Joe, my husband,
who has taught me to live in every language and every country.
He has shown me that love is infinite and unconditional.
Offering me to myself, he encourages me to follow
my dreams, passions, laughter, and desires.
He is one of my most fun playmates and my dearest beloved.*

*To Eric, my mischievous son,
who likes to hide behind doors to scare me to death
so we can laugh and laugh. He settles in next to me,
opening my heart to love, then soars like an eagle
and teaches me about wild and crazy adventures.
He is my other fun playmate.*

In Gratitude

Many thanks to my amazing husband, Joe, and fabulous son, Eric, who inspired me not only at the start but through all the rewrites and a crashed hard drive. To Taylormark Dallas, who retrieved every bit of the material from my computer. To my dear friends Lisa Sziklas and Melissa Weiner, who patiently prodded and encouraged me at breakfast meetings. To Craig Smith, my beloved friend who took many walks with me and held my hand as I talked through problems and solutions. To my editor, Ellen Kleiner, for her very excellent suggestions, patience, and for shepherding me through the entire book-making process. To Janice St. Marie, for her superb artistic eye that created everything from nothing. To Brad Wilson, for sending me the gorgeous photo that became the cover image.

Contents

Days Of the Seasons   9

    We Must Live   11
    Summer Sundays   12
    Noon Whistle   13
    Blackberries   14
    Grandmother   15
    Hoo Hoo   16
    My Children   17
    Metamorphosis   18
    I Am   19
    Waiting For Grace   20
    Tragedy: Susan Smith   21
    The Well   23
    Jealousy   24
    Restless Nocturne   25
    Sadness   28
    Season Of Melancholy and Vultures   29
    Pain   31
    Insomnia   32
    Melancholy   33
    Paris In February   35
    Aging   36
    Clouds   39
    Wind In the Aspens   40
    Winter Storm   42
    The Coming Of Light   43
    Friendship   44
    Time   45
    Harmonic Minor   47
    Father's Day   48
    Autumn Call   50
    The Afternoon   51

Eugenia Cycle — 53

    Russian Woman — 55
    Ode For Gina L. — 56
    Ode To a Pianist — 65

Silhouette In The Dark — 71

    Apotheosis — 73
    Healing — 75
    The Rabbit — 77
    A Tree Blooms In the Heart Garden — 78

Madwoman Cycle — 79

    Madwoman — 81
    The Women's Circle — 82
    The Journey — 83

Love Poems — 85

    The Wind — 87
    First Encounter — 88
    Winter Love — 89
    Tonight I Think Of Him — 90
    Dream Catcher — 91
    Rain and Rain — 92
    Heartblood — 93
    Faraway Love — 94
    The Heart's Tempest — 95
    At Midnight — 97
    Love Is Transparent — 98

Desert Cycle   99

    Creation   101
    Drought   104
    The Storm   107
    Rain   115

Odes   117

    Ravens   119
    Ode For Cathy   124
    June Love   134
    Possessed   137
    Bees   142
    Living   147
    Eric   151

    About the Author   155

Days Of the Seasons

We Must Live

We must live—

Let us embroider
silver starlight
all around the pockets
of our hearts
to guide us through
the twilight
and illuminate the night.

Let us sit silently
and still on the shore,
throwing our names
letter by letter
into the shimmering water
to be eaten
by tiny darting fish,
leaving us naked
and free.

Let time weave
garlands of flame
to crown the lineage
of our eternal beauty,
leaving us standing,
dreaming of miracles,
beacons
at the far end
of the known world.

Summer Sundays

On summer Sundays
we wore black patent leather shoes
and immaculate hand-smocked dresses
held out by scratchy petticoats.

In church, the fans
painted with faded pictures of Jesus,
that Jesus with long, curly hair,
waved slowly,
languorously,
leaving us enervated and limp
from the stifling heat, as we all,
with sweating, white-gloved hands,
began to stick to the hard wooden pews.

Our skirts wilted
as the starch melted,
and our socks drooped,
growing damp,
as we sat transfixed
by the mysteries of ecstatic stories
and mesmerized by the jewel-colored windows.

Noon Whistle

At noon, the factory whistle would blow,
rising up all the way from town
through the woods and fields—
the only punctuation
in the hot summer days
that went on and on,
steaming and slow,
filled with dust and music.

Blackberries

The blackberries ripened in June,
hanging heavy on old thorny vines.
We ran to the farthest reaches
of the fields,
by the periwnkle blue morning glories, barefoot,
our feet summer-calloused like thick leather,
startling birds,
which rose with great wings flapping.
The dogs barked at bees and chased rabbits.
We each clutched a large bowl
in our grubby fingers,
aware of our importance as gatherers.

Hours later, as the heat buzzed around us
and the day went quiet,
we returned,
our bowls full,
quarrels forgotten,
our fingers and mouths stained purple,
our eyes shining
with the secrets we had shared.

Grandmother

She never was the same after
her husband died in Brazil.
I remember that summer
because I was given
a new pink wastepaper basket,
an early birthday present,
just before the shrill ring
startled us.
After the call, everyone spoke
in tears and whispers.
I was afraid and spent hours
sitting by that pink wastepaper basket.
Now when I see it,
I remember the suffocating summer heat,
the viscous quicksand mud from the rains,
and most of all, the pall
of mute sorrow that entered the house
through the small black telephone
on the hall table.

Hoo Hoo

Every Thursday, when I was a child,
we had dinner at my grandmother's house.
Later, after college, I moved to London
to sing opera. It wasn't until I was in Barcelona
where my grandmother visited me,
all angles and elegant pastel dresses,
that I understood the sadness
she drowned with bourbon.
I saw her anguished expression
reflected in the amber liquid in her glass
as she told me about the shock therapy she'd had
when the grief from her husband's death
began to choke her, how even now she didn't
want to be alive. Nothing eased the pain
like bourbon, Jim Beam with water on the rocks.

In Barcelona she talked to me.
It was the bourbon talking, she told me.
That was when I fell in love with her.
Later, when I returned to the States,
at our house on Tuesdays,
at the club on Sundays after church,
I watched Hoo Hoo's happy mask
crumble into despair as the bourbon worked her,
took her away somewhere,
leaving sharpness and despair,
her voice shrill and mean.

I just sat there and held her
as we both remembered Barcelona.

My Children

Two times my body quickened,
my breasts swaying
like ripening summer corn,
my skin glowing,
my belly tightening
to cradle new life.
I dreamed of spring,
of vibrant life
and trees thick with fruit.
My eyes grew soft and watchful
as my body curved around
the life blossoming inside my womb.
I smelled of honey milk
sweated from my rose nipples,
and moist earth rising from
between my legs.

My children were never born—
they rested only a short time inside my body
before continuing their journeys onward.
When I bled,
my children floated away
in purple shrouds.
Afterward I felt a strange seeping wound
that secretly bled sadness in my heart.
I knew they had gone and
a part of me with them.

Metamorphosis

I never tried to be the same as everyone else.
I suffered as my tribe
bit me to fit their mold.

My lineage
grew too tight,
encasing me,
suffocating me.

Like a great blue crane,
I burst
into the sky,
breaking the clouds apart,
never to return.

I Am

I am all I've got.
I, who am made of metal,
earth, and sea,
refuse to sever my wings
and hand them to anyone.
I can wait.

My friends tell me I am
an uncomfortable friend.
Certainly my family finds me uncomfortable.
My friends say I am always
flying off mountains.

Truth—
I know its penalty.
Truth is the talisman I hold against the world.

This world fears honesty;
white lies and niceness are deemed comfortable.
Look what happens to the honest ones,
Martin Luther King and Gandhi.

Comfort has no value for me.
I am not nice.
I want to wear translucent skin,
vulnerable, unashamed skin,
and walk naked in this world.

Waiting For Grace

Her first child, a daughter, lived only a few hours.
She had sons until her marriage burst open.
She planted a rose garden, alone. Waiting

for someone to come to her in that big house.
Three someones came and another daughter,
making her believe in miracles. Now

they all have gone, miracles turned to chimeras.
Age has planted lines in her face.
The roses still bloom every summer.

Tragedy: Susan Smith

She said a black man did it,
tears rolling down her pale white face.
And we bought it,
fueled by young black men
as a metaphor for crime,
sustaining the myth of family
as the safe harbor.

The toy race-car gripped the nation,
the horror of a stranger caught our hearts,
even though statistics tell us
that children are abducted by family members.

She gave CNN a home video
of the eldest child's birthday party.
She asked them to play it over and over.
Every parent in America had sobbed,
seeing those beautiful children,
surrounded by bright paper, eating cake.
CNN broadcast that party video
until it was chiseled into our hearts.

Later, we learned
there was a letter.
The letter said he loved her
but not the children.
So she killed them.
Medea with no purpose,
only hubris.

Murder.

Mothers across America are in shock.
"As a mother of two children, my heart is breaking."
"She could have put those children up for adoption."

This is a community of color,
gone from yellow ribbons of hope
to sludge green grief and vermilion anger,
to prayer vigils, the black community
praying with the white.

Those two babies drowned,
strapped in their car seats;
the maroon car filled with water,
their tiny lungs filled with water.
All sank to the bottom of that murky lake
and settled heavily.
A final sigh.

The Well

I have taken many journeys
to sit at the shore of myself.

There at the edge, I float
scented flowers on the water
to perfume my life.

Jealousy

Liquid green,
biting my liver
until my eyes spill.
Stinking bile,
crocodile tears.
Putrid pus,
destroyer and annihilator.
A twisted pathway,
leading to hatred
and a hollow heart.

I kiss the serpent's tongue, become bloated
        with poison,
     irrational
     and completely blind.

This slow death
shrivels
and desiccates
all life
from the inside out.

Restless Nocturne

In the depths of summer
a moth reaches for the moon,
a mad brutal flight.
What am I looking for?
I am that moth
flying blindly to the cold moon,
so opulent and enticing.
My lungs are bursting
as I strain,
covered in black sweat,
to reach my goal.
I cannot find what I
am searching for.
I cannot find
what I want.

Deep in the jungle
of my twisted shadow longings,
the moon is dark and
the torrid night silent.
The only sound ripping the stillness
is my tumultuous heart
as I struggle to forget my dead.
I bury my tubes of sorrow
deep into the moist, loamy earth.

I am too sad to cry,
too eroded to defy my need.
Inside me there is an upheaval
of enormous proportions.
Incurable restlessness
claws at my dissatisfaction,
unleashing the terrible thundering
of a furious storm.
Blood-red lightning flashes

in a strange, silent sky;
the jagged banners,
heralding arcane gods
of forgotten mythology,
pierce my reason.
I am numb.
There is no way
to mitigate the primal force
at work in me.

The world ends;
the world begins.
It is all the same.
Creation gallops through me.

I want to know what can't be known.
I want to hear the infinite
ice crystal voices of the stars.
My longing to ingest,
to sublimate
and annihilate my mortality,
is unbearable—
the anarchy of the incarnate.

My spirit teases and intoxicates me,
and I reach for a summit
that is only a wisp,
a passing thought
without substance.
I have beaten the hollow drum
until my hands bleed,
and still I drum.
I will find answers
in the repetition,
behind the monochrome monotony.

Blue rain falls on me,
staining me like ink,
wrapping furious lamenting
in my dripping hair.
White rain
falls like caresses
on my trembling.
Rain, sweet rain
anoints my body,
baptizing my existence.

Take me into the depths,
into the dream-sung caverns.
Transform me.
Illuminate me.
Console me.

Make me new—
still my longing,
the awful gnawing,
in the regenerative water-song.
In the eye of the tempest,
I lay down
and I sleep.

As one door closes,
another opens.

Sadness

Yesterday,
waves of sadness crashed against me,
all-night loneliness galloped across me,
smashing the granite walls
I had put around myself.
Then the warm rain fell,
washing away the residue.
Today, the holes in my heart
are filled with summer rainwater.

Season Of Melancholy and Vultures

I came here suddenly,
and found myself
wound
in yards
      and
          yards
of black filmy fabric,
suffocating.

Melancholy clings to me
like old stale smoke.
The young sun has been pierced
and extinguished.
The salamander's tongue of fire
has scorched my eye
and singed my hair,
leaving a stench in the air.

Whose sharp teeth bit me
until they drew blood
and then
fed on my despair?
A parasite
claws open old forgotten wounds,
ripping away the protective covering
of my bruised heart.

What is the antidote
to this dripping darkness,
this water torture
of my heart?
I want more,
much more.
I can see my image
in this pool of tears.

Like a peacock,
I gaze
at my reflected beauty.

When the Lady of Shalott looked
in her mirror,
it broke
and set her free.
I am that lady,
backwards:
still imprisioned.
I am not satisfied.
Sometimes I am too vulnerable
and life aches.

Pain

Pain is laying waste to my heart.
Winds howled in the vast night,
until I lay slivered on the stone altar.
All that is left of me is pain
dancing naked with the sun.

Insomnia

I do not sleep easily.
Life marches through me
as if taking meaning from my blood
until, trembling with exhaustion,
I give up.
Relinquishing the worry,
the racing thoughts
that entice and seduce me
far into the night,
I vanish into sleep.

Melancholy

My heart
has enfolded itself
in winter colors,
heavy,
pregnant,
and close.
One bird,
an arrow misshot
from the bow
of opulent summer,
streaks across the muted landscape.
Melancholy clutches
at me,
despair
as sharp
as blood-red
pomegranate wine.

Vague memories drift by—
I can't hold on to them.
They are dead,
wispy fragments,
long ago sucked dry.
They remind me of
my mortality.

I want to fly
high
and far.
I want to tear away
these cutting stones
of depression
and hurl them
into the distance,
to stifle

the shrill songs.
I have smashed
the mournful bell
of my ancient dried-up longings,
fingernails scraping glass,
passionless mirages
that leave me wanting.

And yet,
somewhere inside,
I want to wrap up
in this autumnal sadness,
letting the desiccated husks of old memories
pass through,
and rest
before winter.

Paris In February

Paris in February
shimmers
beneath a sullen gray winter sky.

I never mind the rain
in Paris,
and am glad
when those
wearied by sodden days
and saddened by mustard-yellow skies
stay away.

Paris is my refuge,
empty and melancholy.
I hug the worn streets.
Here I can feel,
rumbling deep in the hibernating city,
my heart beating with passion.

Aging

Looking at myself in the mirror,
I see life etchings
chiseled around my eyes
and necklaces of time
hanging heavy on my neck.

I thought I would be young forever;
the ads told me so.
I forgot that time was seeping away from me
drop by drop, imperceptibly
sculpting my body into new and strange shapes,
exchanging youthful vitality
for a history
filled with old jewels
and prickly discomfort.
Middle age now
questions my youthful certainty.
I feel gawky
seeing my dreams evaporate,
being stretched thin by unfolding visions.

In which country did I leave those
tender hopes?
On which train racing through which forest
did I forget my earlier loves,
naively believing I would return
and time would have stood still?

The blazing height of summer is upon me,
leaving only longing remembrances
of shimmering spring,
new fire igniting
tiny blue flowers
in naked fertile soil.

I knew the rose would open,
and leave petals falling on the grass.
I knew I would smell in the burning summer sun
the red-flowered spice of autumn,
and wear the sharp sour wind of winter
in my once-dark hair.

Then I will be the silent one
who no longer suffers—
sweet mortality.
My destiny was to touch the stones,
to taste the wind,
to love, to be loved,
and then to leave,
to say goodbye.

I wonder why I had this life.
Which of my threads wove into the mountains,
the seas, the aspen trees,
into the very center of life?
Who conspired with me,
breathing the air I breathed,
until they wrapped their own life around them
and strode out into the world?

Life, the continuum that binds all together.

Will my atoms go forth to form a new galaxy?
Do they swirl around the earth,
falling from the wind into loamy faraway fields?
Do they rest lightly beneath the desert stars?

It all comes back to my being afraid
to give up my unlined skin and walnut hair,
my firm, sleek muscles.
Nothing comes without a price.

Days demand sacrifices;
months and years are bartered
by gravity's constant pull.
And so I pay for my life with my life.

Clouds

Clouds,
press your gray weight
down on me.
My flesh cleaves
deeply
to the fecund earth,
the source.
My spirit
soars beyond the clouds,
effervescent and
unfettered,
into the stars.

Wind In the Aspens

Ancient people thought birds
flew to the moon in winter...

When the birds soared away up to the moon,
wind rushed through the aspens,
sounding like a raging ocean.
The snow came in bursts,
settling on the bare branches,
resting there in profound revelation.

When the birds flew to the moon,
the world became silent...

I had grown mistrustful of all the noise,
the rushing around in relentless pursuit of chimeras.

I welcomed that silence
of winter swirling around me,
transforming all the clatter and the bustle,
stopping traffic, forcing me inside,
until I could finally hear again.
I floated between the northern
and southern seas.

When the birds flew to the moon,
they took away the light...

Darkness covered the earth,
sucking daylight inside itself,
leaving impossible stillness.
Night folded me inside
igloos made of black holes.
I sank gratefully into those huge drifts
and gave away my restlessness.
Here the dance was slow,

drawing me imperceptibly into
that place where rivers converge,
where countries unite.

When the birds flew back from the moon,
the night stayed wrapped around me...

Through long hours I looked out
from the vast and immobile window
that had become my country.
I laid time out, patiently
drawing the boundaries of my land.
I sent my ambassadors out
to trade and bring back provisions.
I built great cities with stones of silence
and mortar of stillness.

When the birds flew back from the moon,
everything had changed for me.

Winter Storm

I ask you: Does the wind blow fiercely
through your restlessness
as you commit the impossible task
of counting each and every star?

Those stars shine balefully
off the stark branches coated in ice,
where the winter storm howled in fury,
beating the silence out of the trees.

Did you hear the constellation's cries
as you turned away from me,
from all of us, wanting to be dead,
gathering up your meager choices in your hands?

What about that storm with sleet
lashing the mountains sideways
until a crack formed where days fell through
and a tiny window opened?

I ask you: Was is here you saw yourself?
Did you grab hold of that tiny sliver of light
to halt your inexorable slide,
returning to us in the ragged night?

We all welcomed you back.

The Coming Of Light

Suddenly, like
sharpened teeth,
light bit into the darkness,
splintering unity,
penetrating life's marrow.
Thus began a siege of separation.
Blood dripped from the stars
as battles of illusion
were fought in ignorance.
The light bored tiny holes
into the stony hardness
of life and death,
stringing the two together
into long swaying strands
of shimmering beads.
Reality took a thousand years to cross the desert.

Ask no more.
Wounded to death
but still living,
become the lance,
become the arrow.

Friendship

A bud,
perfectly formed,
has begun to bloom,
opening slowly,
carefully,
its sweet perfume
scenting the dawn.
The petals unfold,
mesmerizing the morning
with waves of shimmering color.

At the heart of this rose
is the heart of a friend.

When our hearts touched,
you wove a color in the tapestry
of my life,
never to be repeated,
never to be replaced.

You live in the deepest part of me,
remembered in every breath.

Time

I fell out of time,
returning to slowly strangle,
hung by appointments,
commitments, get-togethers,
and everyone who wanted to banquet on my liver.
I was torn in too many directions
by pleasures and desires
until I was hopelessly spent.
I never realized the need to recognize
that passion brings suffering,
that too much really
is too much.
I was happy to step outside
and let time run right by me.
No longer ensnared
in my own frantic race,
I reveled in newfound freedom,
utterly devoid of my madness.

This year I will turn away
from the restless cacophony
that chitters endlessly inside me
and make friends with time.
I will not squander time's gifts
until I lie ragged and panting on the ground.

I will create wild bouquets of scented time,
wrapping the stems in silver conflict,
plucked root by stubborn root
until no more linger within me.
I will seal my extravagant bouquets
with decisions that were not made lightly
and offer them up
to the night winds as they blow through me,
and to my dear heart friends

who held me close throughout,
reminding me to strive for the exceptional
while letting the mundane trickle away.

I now give you the gift of time,
to remember your own inner wisdom—
to turn away from time-draining, mind-numbing
pleasures and strive for that which is higher.

Harmonic Minor

To Tim

"More light! More light!"
Goethe said before he died.

He must have been thinking about you.

I am touched
by your presence,
your grace of being,
your love of the unfathomable.
I am touched
by all the times
we have sat together
in that vast place
between the sixth and seventh,
sharing our lives,
like a rich, fragrant burgundy.

Father's Day

At dawn,
    when the hawk
        soared high
            into the morning,

dropping a seed
    into the moist
        and fertile soil
            of an unknown continent,

light was born,
    blinding,
        more transcendent
            than ever seen before.

I never thought
    to wonder
        if the changes
            in me

would transform you,
    as you soared higher
        in the evening sky, plunging
            like a newly sharpened blade

into the dew-soaked meadow,
    slicing the tall yellow
        grass, hidden from sight.
            We never heard

the bell sound,
    sweeter than love.
        I didn't think
            to say: Remember

who you are now,
> before you raised your tawny eyes
>> to the heavens,
>>> floating away

sleek as smoke,
> golden feathers trailing
>> like medieval banners.
>>> Have you ever felt such joy,

leaving behind all that
> to become a gardener for immortality?
>> I don't want you
>>> to go back,

but to gather up your past,
> to be more than content
>> giving your heart away
>>> more every day,

knowing that love
> brings sorrow
>> and burnishes your soul
>>> to reshape you.

Your seed pierced deep
> into the waiting earth,
>> rending you into pieces
>>> and renewing the universe.

The first breath of creation
> had long waited for this moment,
>> freeing you to be more
>>> than you ever thought possible.

Autumn Call

Autumn called to me
this morning,
in a whisper,
"Come outside,
and see the changes
in the land!"

The Afternoon

The luminous afternoon stretched out.
A bird sang;
the razor-sharp note
split the silence into cerulean ribbons.
Ominous clouds,
fecund with heaviness,
pushed aside the last sliver of blue,
obliterating the light.
The day disappeared;
all sound ceased.

Let us firmly grasp
our dreams of joy,
left fallow and forgotten
in the drought-parched fields.
Let us relinquish loss
and notice the day swirling around us.
Can we allow the detritus of separateness
to trickle through our fingers with our regrets
and dissolve in the deep cold water?
Let us awaken,
knowing at the end we are safe.
Let us, finally, plant the glimmering seeds
of our rare and uncharted lineage of light
into the rich and waiting soil.

Eugenia Cycle

Russian Woman

When I look at you, I see you radiant,
the long white days of frozen northlands
turned to molten gold by the sun's hands.

I see multicolored ribbons of laughter beside your eyes,
twining around the Maypole, ensuring fertility,
inviting the great sword of eternity to the dance.

I see a child, buffeted by sea breezes,
transformed into a woman, shining and proud,
who stood her ground, even as waves spat around her.

I see a woman made of stars, who ate the wind,
leaving her homeland, weaving anguished despair
into sinuous music that sailed into a newer world.

Ode For Gina L.

That day,
that night,
raven-haired woman,
your journey
began,
light streaming
as spring
strode
into
the white
winter-weary city,
commanding
"Look at me!"—
the resonant voice
vibrating
swiftly
and confidently
through
the
razor-sharp
antenna
of the
Golden Spire,
a defiant lance
thrusting into the heavens,
piercing
the snow-laden clouds,
cutting open
the bitter cold,
screaming
for the equinox
to return.
Ice,
thick as grief,
splits,

the echo
thundering
in the cracks
of recalcitrant winter,
slicing
a jagged
hairline fissure,
churning up
calcareous winter
on the River Neva.
That
dreadful crack,
splintering
the harsh,
unrelenting
hold
on the great land,
is the edge
of Death
sucking away
the bitter cold,
darkness
making way
for the triumph
of new light.

The young sun
has risen
and becomes strong.
Once upon a time
there was a girl.
Woman of water,
fluid woman,
the sea
glittered
in your eyes.

You
were drenched
with salt air,
dressed
in sea foam,
Venus reborn.
The ocean
sang
gently
in your bay.
How silent
were the rocks,
the great sentinels,
worn smooth,
serene,
by the washing
of the waves.
The rugged,
farseeing rocks,
pulverized by time
and
tides,
filled the beaches.
Water,
the humid lifeblood,
sang
through the city
at your birth.
This remote coast,
covered in darkness,
impassable
in winter,
surrendered first
to the Vikings,
when Rurik
crossed

the huge waters
in his dragon-prowed
wooden ship,
oars
digging deep
into
the frigid waters,
buffeted by
turbulent storms,
sailing finally
onto
the outstretched shores
of the
new homeland.

Later,
fierce Mongols
roamed,
conquering
the vast northern steppes,
wrestling
the fetid bog
from Sweden.
Peter the Great
founded
his capital,
built
on the bones
and mortared
with
the thick hot blood
of Swedish prisoners,
laboring,
perishing,
becoming the foundation
of the

glittering
great capital,
Sankt Peterburg.
Bones
upon
bones,
as the tsars
reigned
then
were interred,
those bones
crumbling,
blood
flowing
like rich wine,
bathing
the dreary
streets,
reflected
in the haze
of the fiery
sunset,
manifest
in red banners
of purges
and ideology.
Blood streamed
into canals,
into
the River Neva.
Keening Hunger
and
her gaunt sister,
Starvation,
occupied
the weary city,

Petrograd,
Leningrad,
St. Petersburg.

Child of the White Nights,
you came to tell
your story,
as you
preserved
the memory
of your lineage.
Look!
You danced,
you sang,
you spun your thread
in a city
of bridges,
until you became
a bridge
between
the ancient,
familiar land
and
the New World.
This bridge,
huge
and
golden,
was built on
conquered fear
and mighty courage.

Laughing woman,
polished transparent
by love,
by loss,

by life,
through
the splintered sounds
of a raging tempest,
you
left
everything
behind,
taking
only
the hands
of your husband
and
your child.
How full
are those hands
that
hold
your childhood,
your beloved,
and
your only son.
Countless bouquets
of music
have poured
from these hands,
falling
like meteors
to nourish
emptiness
and
eternity.

Look,
your face
is etched

with ecstasy.
You
are
a flash of truth,
beautiful
and
victorious.
Stop
for one moment
as you move
through
the stony
labyrinth
of your life,
and in
that profound
silence
ask,
"What is real?"
as you
search
for the ineffable
and unknowable.
Does
that flame
sear your heart,
until
it opens,
singing?
Do you
seek
solitude?
Have you
heard
the clarion
sounds

of the stars'
hearts
beating,
whirling
through
the fathomless sky,
when
your heart
burns
with passion
where all yearning
and ambition
are stilled?

Only
music
remains,
quivering notes
resounding
with clarity
and brilliance
through
that solitude,
until
you awaken,
astonished,
as
the universe
breathes
through you,
revealing
your exquisite
beauty.

Ode To a Pianist

Supple hands
shaped
like roses,
sculpting
silence
with long,
slender
fingers,
leaving
and returning,
returning
and leaving,
notes
pounding,
shivering,
dripping
like warm spring rain
into the world,
transparent,
silvery and wild,
transmuting
the darkness.
Each note,
thinner
than an arrow,
more powerful
than a tempest,
reaching
into
the heart
to draw
clear sweet water
back into
this world.
Hundreds

of tiny
golden notes,
sinuously
piercing
the flesh,
softening
stone,
bleeding,
weeping,
exulting.

Oh,
these serpent
hands
that slide
through
thunder,
darting
like hummingbirds
into
the atmosphere!
What complex
action
is the touch
of a fingertip
on a key.

One touch
etches
sound
into silence,
a shimmering light
for those
who
have
lost all hope,

a clear
beacon
for the heart
to follow,
a caution
to forget
banal
and
mundane cares
that steal
our lives
away
forever.

Time
ceases
to cut away
at the flesh
of our living,
but
leaves
to hibernate,
suffused
by the heady scent
of the music.

Those
blue granite
hands
crash down,
seizing
the keys,
demanding
more,
denying
Death's power,

whirling and
stomping.
Sound
overflows
into the silence
as
all the fingers
create
a new world,
a refuge
from
loss
and
despair,
where
the heavy
worn armor
encasing
our hearts
can be left
outside,
hanging
on wooden pegs,
as we
step
through
the exultation
of sound,
naked
and vulnerable.

Oh!
Here
feeling
is alive
and so intense

that
we ache
with wonder.
Life and
death
dance
a pavane
together,
with measured,
graceful,
intricate steps.

We are
burnished
and
preserved,
safe
in the center.
The music
issuing
from your hands
restores
our vision,
clouded
with uncertainty
and
weariness,
establishes
truth,
illuminates
the fearsome
night,
stills our longings
and draws
the poison
from our ambitions.

Silhouette In The Dark

Apotheosis

All of you
snatched parts of me,
wrapping me viciously
in oblique shrouds
of violence.
What were you seeing
in my little body,
bleeding and hurt,
as you tore off your morsel
and left?
You were cannibals,
eating away at my body
to ease your pain
and your hopelessness.
The more you ate,
the more you craved.

I became insane,
numb to your wretched
devouring of my flesh,
my heart.
Polluted and lost,
I wandered for years
in twisted corridors of pain,
stinking of dank depression,
a river of shame
running sluggish and deep
beneath my hidden labyrinth
of self-hatred and despair.
I became my minotaur.
I mutilated myself.
My bruised heart
burst into a million shards
lying rusted in oily water,
until rising

from the primordial untouched depth,
spurred on by
the flame
that never died,
having drunk deeply
from the sacred grail
of my soul,
I said, "No!
No more!"

I raised my shield of power
and reflected Myself
to myself.
I gathered the broken
pieces of my heart,
weaving a banner
of steady courage
and shimmering love.
I arose,
like the phoenix,
born anew
inside my own heart,
singing the song of the morning.

Healing

I wanted to hide
from the world,
to pretend
that I was so strong
nothing could hurt me.
I wanted to forget
the agony.

At times I wasn't sure
I wanted to stay alive.
I wanted to veil my face
and dance with death.

I wanted love
at any price:
cold love,
hard love,
toxic love.

I wanted to fill up
that hollow place inside me
with anything.
I wondered if that emptiness
would finally coat me in bitumen
and consume me.

I wanted my life to be different—
and we all know that changes
come from inside us.
I had to hurl myself
into my future.
I stitched the slashed pieces
back together slowly,
painstakingly.

It isn't always simple to live in this world.
It helps to be gentle and kind
and quit looking for the easy way out.

The Rabbit

What is this tiny unremembered thread
of pain that tears at me?
My heart is pierced by
the strong cruel talons
of the sorrow hawk.
The pain is so sharp
that I am gasping,
my breath taken away.

They locked me
into this nightmare
I had forgotten.
Agony unstraps my tears.

Wash me,
wear away
the stone.

Remind me...
Remind me...

A Tree Blooms In the Heart Garden

I am alone in the death agony of my heart;
this is my resurrection.
I am too exhausted to mourn anymore.
My tears are filled with iron pain.

I don't want to eat your bread and salt.
I cannot wear your brand of salvation.
It burns me,
inscribing acid etchings on my soft flesh,
carving into my heart.

You cannot touch me.
I have stripped you away
and am naked.
I have walked until my feet bled
to leave the tangled chaos
you planted inside me.
I have let your anger slip away,
forgotten and dismembered,
into the deepest abyss,
decomposing into impotence.
I have ripped out the fear
that was clinging in my crevasses.
Your silicone-coated lies are silent now,
shattered in the red dust.

My empty spaces are green with new growth.
My hand is gently holding
the rooting seed of my future.

Madwoman Cycle

Madwoman

I am the madwoman
who sits in the center,
disrupting dreams
and troubling life.

I am a power station
flinging my raw electricity
at the cardinal points.
I am the amber scorpion
stinging myself to death.

I hide in the churning darkness
of primal intuition,
of forbidden yearnings.
I crave the hot bright blood
of innocence.
I am Kali's handmaiden.
I am Sleeping Beauty, unawakened.

I live in freefall
and stand in the doorsill.
I lead
to annihilation and
to self-renewal.
I offer myself as sacrifice to
unlock the gateway
into the labyrinth of
womanhood.

The Women's Circle

In the circle of my grandmothers
my place is waiting.

Circles of women,
circles of return,
circles of silent strength.

How do I enter?
How do I immerse myself
in the flow
until,
sanctified,
I can see the doorway
in the midst of the interwoven dreaming
of all these women?

The Journey

I have wandered in the desert
until my feet are bruised
and I am too weary to move.
My lips are cracked and there is no water.
I am left alone with myself.
I have nowhere to hide
in this bleak place.

I see your face in the huge moon
and see you shimmering in the heat of the day.
You are the keeper of the ancient creation hymns,
and know the secret passages
to the River beneath the river.
You are the Old Woman,
the One Who Knows,
who can sing life into my exhausted being.

Hold my hand—I am lost.
Lead me into the depths of the desert of my life,
and teach me the power of myself.
At the edge of the two worlds
I can regain myself and run free
until, speeding past the night,
I touch my soul and hold us
in a tight embrace.
Then will my voracious thirst
be finally assuaged.

Here I will gather stars
and sing my yearning and my despairing loneliness,
letting my wild fierce songs
pour over my bleached luminous bones.

Love Poems

The Wind

The wind roared into my heart,
a hot mistral
swirling through me,
driving me insane.

I want to bite
into you
and drink your essence.

Oh! You,
my lover,
my heart.

First Encounter

Alabaster lover,
of what do you dream
as you gaze deep into the continent
of your longing?
In your reverie
you are provocative,
primal and austere.
You are the beginning of creation,
chaste and holy,
erotic and sexual.
I want to touch you,
slide my fingers
across the nape of your neck
until you rest your head
on my breast
and listen to the secrets whispered
from my heart.

Winter Love

Remote and inaccessible,
I cannot reach you.
You are far away,
too far.
A mirage,
you vanish in the frozen wasteland
when I approach.
I am exhausted
traversing
your inhospitable boundaries,
never getting closer,
never getting warmer.

Who are you?
What are you?
What do you have to do with me
that I, drugged
on some potent vision,
leave my birthplace
to follow your jagged paths,
whipped by your furious storms?
In your remote and foreign landscape
I ache with a loneliness
that rips my heart.
What kind of love
is this winter love?

Tonight I Think Of Him

Tonight I think of him and feel despair.
Like a great white swan, he spread his wings
and flew from me. His wing beat tore my heart.

The soft night cuts through these arms that held him.
The night is huge without him.

I see his bright eyes in each star.
I love him
and at times he loved me.

How intensely I desired him
and ate his kisses like succulent exotic fruit.

I am afraid I have lost him.
Pain flows like blood, unstaunched
from cold wounds ripped open by love's claws.

Dream Catcher

Man with the eyes of dawn,
you surprised my heart.
I had waited so long
I forgot you were coming.

Man made of starfire,
your love pierced my heart.
I opened myself like a promise
and let you enter.

Together, we embraced
as the arrow of the night passed,
still flaming,
and the day folded into us.

Rain and Rain

Rain falls,
putting out the sun,
sheathing the day
in black unnatural night.

I ache for you,
so far away.

Rain falls,
unleashing chaos,
ravaging the trees,
shrieking around the long day.

You swallowed my heart whole,
and I am left wounded.

Rain falls,
rain, then rain,
just rain bleeding
into the earth.

I think of you,
your dreamsong face,
your eagle-flight soul.

Through our love,
thunder lies silent in my hand,
lightning illuminates my heart.
And I am left trembling in the richness of loving.

Heartblood

The look in your eyes
pricked my heart,
until I bled from loving.

I have lost myself.
I hear you everywhere:
at the edge of day emptying into night,
in the shadows of night reassembling into day.

Descent into vertigo.
Before, I was certain;
now, I am uncertain.
Through love's ache
I have a fierce preoccupation with living.

Faraway Love

You are too far away.
My thoughts cover you
in a net of silver,
weaving you into my dreams.
And still this sullen ache remains.

I remember you lying beside me,
softer than moonlight.
Love shuddered around us,
weaving us into one tapestry.

Man of my heart,
how I miss you.

The Heart's Tempest

I wish you would hold my heart,
I wish you would appear
waiting for me in the desolate desert
of my aching heart.
I wish you would drink my tears
until all my thirst is quenched,
and my burning anguish transformed
by your love.
I wish that you,
the Ship with the White Sails,
would sail into the tempest of my longing
and dissolve me forever.
Can you possibly know the strength of my passion?

If you would just hold my heart
in your warmth,
I would thaw and awaken.
A note, deep inside me,
would sound,
uncharted and wild,
which like a flaming arrow
would pierce into the very essence of life.
All the brittle crystallized fragments of me
would shatter into pieces,
leaving me vulnerable and real.
My heart would dance recklessly,
covered in gritty sea spray,
amidst the haphazardly twisting waves,
leaping, ripping through all the deadness.
Ruthless destroyer,
brilliant creator,
dissolving and evolving into infinity
until, filled and overflowing,
daring to be courageous,
I grow into your love.

Hold me tightly,
so tightly that I forget
and unzip my lacerations.
Hold me tightly,
so tightly that we weld together,
soar
far beyond the boundaries of passion,
and unite at the crossroads
of madness.
Absorb me! Ingest me!
And together let us find
that silent place
in the midst of the hurricane of our hearts,
where matter falls into nothingness.
It is here that I find you,
beloved you,
fierce you.

You already know the secret entrance
into my darkest places.
Let me climb inside with you
and see with your clarity,
gestate in your love.
Here I can lay down my head
and rest my wounded heart.
Here I can give up my weapons
and shed my steel cocoon.

At Midnight

At midnight the world changes.
The night bursts open.

At midnight we become immortal.
Our hearts meet in the garden of stars.

At midnight the nighthawk flies.
Passionate love immolates me.

At midnight the night becomes velvet.
I slide my hand into yours forever.

At midnight dreams are woven.
The crescent moon illuminates our love.

At midnight, star-woven man,
you are mine.

Love Is Transparent

Love is transparent,
riding into the heart,
illuminating this life,
rising far above the mountains
through the infinite sky,
darkening into the purple clouds
of approaching dusk,
into nothing we have ever known.

Captured by your love,
I am ripped apart,
divided,
my dark blood
cascading
until I overflow this world.
I cannot return.

No one ever returns.

Desert Cycle

Creation

In the beginning there was the wind
wailing and cajoling,
echoing hideously,
filling the silence so fully
that it burst into anguished fragments,
which buried themselves,
hiding deep within shaded crevices,
moaning within dusty parched stone.
The gods of the desert rose in glory,
challenging life to take hold
in this harsh, inhospitable land.

"How?" screamed the air,
dropping seed
onto the burning, thirsty soil.

"Where?" shrieked the raven,
blown in on the wind.

The unanswered questions
rose from the desert to linger,
like a stubborn scent,
immutable as the low-toned bell
that tolled the death of Christ.

The earth sang,
vibrant with power,
radiant with beauty,
summoning the rain gods,
who wept in ecstasy,
greening the plains,
filling the lakes,
raising the corn.

In the desert
the fractured silence hummed,
toning a diaphanous thread
into the earth's medicine song,
silvery as the hummingbird's flight,
soft as insects buzzing in the grasses,
free as the mountains soaring into infinity,
weaving supple strands
of sustenance and renewal
into the vibrant desert tapestry.

Light, enthralled by the song, awoke,
detaching itself from the sun
to flow sinuously across the land,
creating shadows hiding mysteries,
reflecting vermillion light onto the shimmering sand.

The mountains, guardians
of ancient memories of origin,
battered by wind, rain, and brutal cold,
cracked and splintered
into fantastic monuments of naked stone,
ochre mesa, and blood-red canyons,
whose etched thick walls
reach far into the vast sky,
consuming the heart,
swallowing fear, echoing the song.

Each grain of sand,
once hard, unyielding stone,
pounded fine
by the relentless elements,
resonated strength and longevity,
a hologram of the original.

So the desert was born
of sweat,
of unbearable heat,
of song,
into unspeakable beauty.

Drought

The drought
is
a spear
thrust
into the desert
that
quivers
and
splits
the universe
in half.
Painful
aching
heat
wells
from
parched
and
wretched
land.

Green
stretched
beyond endurance
turns brown
crisp at the edges
sharp
hot as the fire
of a star's belly
the final flash
of the aurora borealis
a glorious display
a last SOS
heartbreaking
in its beauty.

This
is
the
death rattle
of one life
quietly
and
irrevocably
slipping away
mortality
tumbling
into
immortality.

The trees
scorcherd by the sun
pull their life
inside
and sink their roots
deep
deeper
into the desiccated,
dehydrated earth,
hoping for the miracle
of rain.

Their scent
spicy and
angular
redolent
of the summer monsoon
embraces the air
concealing
the very moment
of life

lost
to the relentless
implacable
rainlessness.

The Storm

The storm
sweeps
over the mountains
gaudy
in the panoply
of fat
black clouds
shrieking
thunders
growling loud
fierce
challenges
stark white
lightning
scorching
the edges
of the roiling
skies
and
not
a
drop
of
rain
falls.

We wait
agony
of expectation
and
longing.
Our desire
raging
exacerbated
by the thick

welcome
scent
of rain.
Ominous
quiet
heavier than
final partings
bolting us
down
to the hairline
at the edge
of despair—
and still
the
rain
does
not
come.

Can
they
who love
sit
patiently
at the center
of the furrow
calmly shaping
the life
that was
always
their own
deaf
to
the whirling
touching
the drenched

topaz presence
planting
plant
after plant
soaring
deep
into
the luminous
earth?
Untouched
by
expectation
the breath
of the heart
raises
the leafage
a presence
of gentle
immutable
power.
Love holds
us all
in thrall.
And
no
rain
falls.

The storm
drills
into
our senses
rooting us
into
immobility.
Our breasts

fall
open
the red rose
striving
to entwine
with
the
white rose.
Trees
bloom
stars
a halo
for
our anguish.
Our
too loud
heartbeats
send
flocks of
butterflies
sparks
to pierce
the
obsidian
sky.
And
still
there
is
no
rain.

My mouth
is dry
my palms
clammy. Oh!

expectation.
I
crave
the end,
begging
for
the promise
of
the molten sky.
I
shiver
as sweat
beads on
my
rubber band–
tight
forehead
burning
in my need
disfigured
by longing
honed
by
the lack
of resolution.

Harpooned
by
the elemental power
I am
oblivious
to my
hatreds
angers
loves
every hair

on end
as
lightning
rips
through the sky.
I ache
to be beaten
into sanity
by
the storm.
Still
no
rain
falls.

Somewhere
in the desert
a scorpion
stings its prey
and
changes
the world
forever.
A flower
blooms
a miracle
that
laces
the day
with
opulent fragrance.
The night
grows
enormous
curving
enveloping.

My
hands
are
shaking.
And
still
rain
does
not
fall.

The storm
passes
through
a great
funeral
cortege
muted boomings
and
sharp
painfully angular
light
displays
searching
for
another place
to
lay down
its
oppressively
heavy burden.
And we
the
waiting ones
are left
exhausted

naked,
not satiated
sweat-drenched
in
the cold
and
empty
silence
comfortless
and
unresolved.

Rain

The wind rested, motionless.
The rain lashed the land.
Minute by minute,
the sky opened wider,
its full unnatural darkness
ripped by jealous lightning
until, overflowing,
the silent rain falls,
satiating the thirsty earth,
filling all wounds.

Odes

Ravens

Ravens,
streaking
like music
across the sky,
lift their powerful wings
to
ride
the thermals
in
the
stillness
of the clouds.

There is much to say about the ravens,
who
drop
like light
detached
from the sun,
like stones
of solitude,
to congregate
at our pond.
They stride
with fierce confidence
across the grass,
like nobility
returning
to an ancient,
ancestral home.

What do they know?
What distant memories
do they hold
of this place?

They declared my garden
a temple
and remain
all
day,
great obsidian black wings unfurled,
splashing
in
the
waterfall.
Their golden eyes
are radiant,
vivid,
wicked
with arcane wisdom.

They rest,
sentinels,
time
standing
motionless.
A lightning flash
rooted,
transformed into stone,
wrinkled with tenderness,
with passion,
enveloping
silence,
stillness,
eternity.

If
you
think
a raven

is
just
a raven,
then
you
miss
the mystery,
the oracle.
Not all life opens outward.
Not all life is visible.

Once
when I was pregnant,
in the hour
of iron,
as
a
tiny
sliver
of glowing light
illuminated the east,
liberating the day,
the ravens arrived
in
great
and
particular
silence.
They
hovered around me,
my guardians,
majestic like planets,
intent
as the color guard
at Buckingham Palace.

When
the baby
slipped away
in
a river
of
blood,
finished with its purpose,
leaving incarnation
without
birth,
leaving me empty,
desolate,
taking
all
the
light,
the ravens remained,
patient,
persevering,
until
my churning grief,
like a hollow drum
beaten dry,
drained
away
into that comforting silence.

Here with the ravens,
I will remember.
Ravens preserve the memory.
Death
arrives
at
great
cost.

The wheel turns,
beginning.
ending,
beginning again.
Did
the ravens
guide my child
on her journey back home?

I saw
those ebony sentinels
fly
to the sun
and
bring back
silence.

The ravens reestablished light in my
land.

Ode For Cathy

Woman of air,
the calm
before the storm,
the eye
of the hurricane,
vast
and silent,
sending
winds
to
sweep
passion,
ecstasy,
and fury
from the stony
mountains
onto the
vast
plains,
you weave
creation songs
and
lace
lilac-edged clouds
into
the tendrils
of your
hair,
plaiting
and
binding reality.
You stood
immovable,
facing
all directions,

communing
impudently
with
the
one who knows
you
completely,
alone
in pure solitude,
highly polished
by time,
shining
like
a love letter,
savoring
freedom,
feasting
on your life
until
your body,
protesting
its lack
of immortality,
went on a rampage
and
said,
"No!
No more!"

Your body
shook you
until
you
awakened
from
the dreaming

and
took a
long
draught
of death's
nectar.

Was
there despair
as your heart
of air,
filled with
the wild
pungent winds
of spring,
caught
fire
and burned
away
until
no air
was left?
Did
you take
the last
turquoise
threads
and
fling them
into
the universe,
howling,
looking
for
the one trick
that would

convince
your body
to return?

God
is easy
to find
in the
languid
air of summer,
but
when
the darkness
folds down
claustrophobically
all
around
you,
clinging
passionately
to you,
so that you,
sweating,
cannot
peel
free,
it is
far more
difficult
to
believe.

Perhaps
this is
why
we don't

close
our eyes.
There,
in that
sharpened
night,
fear
fell
like
silent snow
all around
as
you gathered
the
last
drops of blood
frozen
into
red lilies
and screamed
your life
back
into existence.

Did you fall,
dull-eyed,
to your
bloody
and torn
knees,
embracing earth
before
you
rose,
little
by little,

through
swirling mist,
a new continent,
vast and majestic,
created
from
the lava
of destruction,
welling
up from
extinguished air?

When
you broke
open,
earth seized you.
You went
to
the desert,
walking
and walking,
striding
away
from
your past,
stomping,
stamping,
creating
your present,
dancing
gardens
into existence.
Nourished
by your
scalding
hot tears,

water
of a new life
sinking
into
the dry
desiccated earth,
tapping
and
whirling,
dancing
with both feet
firmly
and fully
on the ground,
a sliver
of your soul
slipped into
the earth,
and knotted,
holding fast,
rooting deeply,
so that earth
rose up
to meet you.
Earth,
the Great Mother,
awakened.
In that
atavistic pounding,
thirstily drinking
the tears
freely given,
she rose
from
deep caverns
beneath

the harsh ground
and entered
the soles
of your feet,
pounding out
pain,
frustration,
and
rage.

Those feet
that
had walked
through
your birth,
your childhood,
into love
and into art,
those feet
that refused
to follow
any more orders,
found
a new beat
and a new rhythm.
Earth
gave back
your heart,
and you gave
yourself
completely
to Earth,
giving
air
a place
to roam,

to live,
to nest.

Your feet
slowly
and deliberately
quieted
their
frantic pounding.
Your rage
coalesced
into jagged peaks
of exquisite beauty,
a nesting place
for golden eagles.

From
within,
you
gave
birth
to clay,
which spilled
from your hands,
soothing
your wounded heart,
accepting
your
obstinate body,
introducing
you
to the stranger
you had become.

You left
behind

the old voices
and ways
as you heard
the soft,
clear voice
coming from
within you.
Be helpless.
Be amazed
as
you surrender
to your
extraordinary beauty.

Woman of air,
woman of water,
I salute you.

June Love

In hot,
dry
June,
my heart tore
and bled.
You held me
tenderly,
softly.
I
loved you,
silent
as a snake,
deeper
than light,
sea-changed.

Passionately
I wanted
to eat
your
dark purple lips
and wrap
myself around
you
until
you rose up
burning,
love's fierce
unapologetic
angel
keeping death
at bay.

My passion
pounds,

waves crashing
against
my frail body
until I am
the sea,
woven with stars,
drying into melodies
and whiplash
anguish.
Kiss me,
I am salt
left at the edge
of the pounding surf.
Taste me,
I am bitter
and mysterious.

I left
my doors
unlocked,
waiting
for you
to enter.
You
swept into me,
an overflowing
river,
melting my heart,
leaving
puddles
of iridescent love
within me.
Sweet ache
of a love-engorged
heart.
Burning.

Desire,
sharper than razors.
I knew
you would come,
a ship
on my horizon,
returning
to harbor,
burning
a beacon
in the night.
Oh! This night
wrongs are
righted
and
darkness is
reconciled
with light.
I am left
feverish,
delirious.
Darling,
do not fear
my love.

Love me.
Love me.
Love me.

Possessed

I am possessed.

Life reached inside
the cave of my heart
and blew it
like
a cloud
into the embrace
of the opalescent moon—
a luminous window
that opens
endlessly inward—
a waterfall
of light
regenerating
my
being.

My blood
was shed
for all,
a mystical
Eucharist.
Drink the torrid blood rain;
the hot blood
births
obelisks,
vertical monuments
to
the
born
and
reborn
sun god,
stealing time

and
locking it
into engraved wheels,
a theft
protested
by
sharp,
stinging
winds
scented
with iron.
Charred
by the noonday sun,
the fundamental
remains
intact.

I choose
to stride
into foreign lands.
I scream
into the night,
a bargain sealed,
a challenge issued.
The granite silence
shatters,
then
reforms
at its core,
infusing
the throbbing dawn
with unspeakable
beauty.
The original is
never again
to

be
repeated;
I am
my original.

I wanted
to carve
myself
into
an icon
of experience
and
history,
multifaceted,
but my diamond flesh
breaks
the chisel.

I cannot
be fragmented.

I am
a sinner.

I am
the whore
of the universe,
engorged with desire,
stinking
of sex.

I am
the Virgin,
translucent green flame,
torch of the courageous,
banner of the intrepid.

My pedestal
was broken
in two
by the sharp teeth
of the turquoise salamander,
keeper of starfire.
Flame
enveloped
my essence.
Sisyphus stole a coal
from the salamander.
No
one
can
steal
my
fire.

I flung my anger
back
to the sky.
Life is
too important
to remain
angry.
My life
is too important
to barter
for transitory comforts.

I demand
the
full
experience.
When

I have consumed
the
final
condensation
of life,
evaporating
into
its
most secret self,
I will walk
through
the rose window
into
the
next
world,
where the present
hangs
motionless.
I will
leap
out of the abyss
of the past
onto
the diaphanous precipice.

If
we
keep
stepping backwards
all
we do
is reignite
the past.

Bees

Here at
the final edge
of day,
the bees
arrived
to drink
at the pond.
Entitled,
oblivious,
they settled
on rocks
at
the water's edge,
drawing
their sun-gilded wings
in
to rest,
a brilliant sea
of yellow and black,
majestic,
like tiny sparks
from the sun
glittering
against the gray stone.

When the wind
warms
with the scent
of summer
and
wraps around
the tender
emerging buds,
I go
to the pond

to meet the bees,
to welcome them back
from their winter journey.

They tumble
through the air
like
tiny arrows
shot
from a far-off bow,
like warriors
reclaiming
their birthright,
singing
their secret music
of power.
I sit with them
in stillness,
in companionable silence,
listening.

My life
is
grander,
fuller
for
their presence.
The cage
around
my heart
bursts open,
exploding
into silver fragments,
absorbed
into shooting stars
to

set
me
free.

Nature saves
my life
with its
utter
and
insouciant
magnificence.

Dropping
like glowing petals,
the bees
rest
on long shaded leaves
that drop
into
the rippling pond—
water
gilded,
stained
gold-pink-orange
by the last
moments
of the sunset.
The undulating pond
becomes
a punctuation
of
the
eternal.

Somehow
the bees know

the exact moment
when day
teeters
over
into the cusp
of dusk,
when the rosy gilt
becomes
mauve
and copper,
signaling
day's end.
At
this
exact
moment,
they rise
and hover
for a brief,
timeless instant,
where
death
rests gently,
a shimmering thread
in life's
complex tapestry,
radiant
and exquisite
in
pulsating completeness.

They depart
like a golden lance,
a constellation moving
into

the gossamer violet
of twilight.

I am left
filled with
deep,
irrepressible
contentment
and gratitude,
embraced
by the moment.
I stand gazing
a long time
at the diminishing horizon
for one
last glimpse
of them.
As the final
pale orange sun
slides away
completely,
I rest
in
unbroken belonging.

Living

Out of
the sharp edge
of loneliness
seep
bituminous tendrils
of longing—
two magnets
sodden
with violent regrets
like fire,
the viscera of desire
aching
again.

Life is
neither fair
nor unfair;
it just is.
Neither kind
nor unkind,
it spins on,
undaunted,
in its time,
dissolving
and renewing
within itself.

Don't
tell
me
how
to grieve
or how
I

must lay aside
my sorrow
and move on,
that
it is time.
(As if time
were a
neat
and tidy package
pristinely prewrapped
for presentation,
like European candies
in their
fantastical,
gorgeous
boxes.)

Goodbye.
Goodbye.
Goodbye.

Somewhere in the universe
a machete
slashed,
biting deeply
into crystal
until a new note,
emerging
from
steaming blood,
sounded,
clear
and
pregnant
with the possibility
of infinite
starry

space.
The noonday sun
pierced
the silence.
The note
grew
big.
Its huge belly
quivered
in the night,
luminous
in the moonlight.

Not
a single vibration
is
lost
to death
or frigid darkness;
all
envelops me
in fecundity,
strengthening
my heart
as
I sleep.
The boundless resonance
wakens
me,
planting
the revolving
music
of the spheres
into
my burning flesh,

baring its teeth,
branding
the song of creation,
a miracle
that
clots
my sadness
and
transmutes
my longing
into
barbarian gold.

Look!
Skimming
the horizon,
the silhouette
of a rising bird.

Eric

Whoever likened a child to a rose
did not have a boy.

Eric is the music of fire
and exultation,
of planets colliding
to create new constellations,
of immense
and unimaginable beauty.
He is the primal sound,
the solitary note
of a diamond arrow
shot far into the sun,
where, smoldering
and coagulating,
he bursts forth,
transmuted
into molten lava,
flowing
like metal...
like magic...
like silence.

Inhaling freedom,
he sings,
trembling with free will,
flung like a comet
across the sky,
exploding black holes
into phosphorescent fireworks
of shooting stars
streaking into infinity.
A phoenix,
Icarus
with wings of flame extended,

streaking across the heavens,
trailing fire
and jubilation,
daring the stars
to race with him.

He is the howling wind
at the beginning of creation,
a tsunami
turbulent with thunder,
flinging lightning bolts
into space,
ripping continents apart,
reconfiguring mountain chains,
defining archipelagos,
filling oceans,
shifting the axis
of the world,
a tempest
tearing into space,
consuming the universe,
rearranging gravity.
Stubborn as stone,
he becomes rain,
falling in sheets,
flooding rivers,
ending droughts,
eroding ancient beliefs.

He is a magician
who transforms the world
into an eclipse of time,
bristling,
slippery,
molten
until, finally consumed

and satiated,
arms stretched above his head,
he
falls
asleep.

Tender,
breath smooth as leaves,
soft as darkness,
sweet as liberation,
all thorns hidden,
he sleeps . . .

A rose.

About the Author

Gina Browning was born in Pittsburgh and grew up in Kentucky. She graduated from Indiana University School of Music and is a singer of classical music. She performs opera and chamber music around the world and currently specializes in new music. She began writing poetry on a dare and found that poetry is a perfect expression for her passionate and exuberant life. Her other passions include gardening, writing, skiing, and overseas travel. Ms. Browning is also the author of the poetry collection *Roses of Heart*. She lives with her husband and son in Santa Fe, New Mexico.

www.ingramcontent.com/pod-product-compliance
Lightning Source LLC
Chambersburg PA
CBHW052048070526
44584CB00017B/2102